THE HOG KILLING

POEMS

GARY COPELAND LILLEY

BLUE HORSE PRESS   REDONDO BEACH, CALIFORNIA   2018

THE HOG KILLING

GARY COPELAND LILLEY

Blue Horse Press
318 Avenue I # 760
Redondo Beach,
California   90277

Cover photo: Wild Hogs near Kennedy Space Center
Public domain (no date).

Editors: Jeffrey and Tobi Alfier
Blue Horse Press logo: Amy Lynn Hayes (1996)

ISBN 978-0692131848

This and other Blue Horse Press Titles may be found at
www.bluehorsepress.com

Other Poetry Books by Gary Copeland Lilley

The Bushman's Medicine Show Lost Horse Press (2017)

High Water Everywhere Willow Books (2013)

Cape Fear Q Ave Press (2012)

Alpha Zula Ausable Press (2008)

Black Poem Hollyridge Press (2005)

The Subsequent Blues Four Way Books (2004)

The Reprehensibles Fractal Edge Press (2004)

To Lillian Camilla Copeland Lilley

Acknowledgements

The Swamp: "The Car is the Crucial Chariot to Rural Culture"

Contents

Day of the Dead

The photos on the wall
above the altar, the ghosts
and their times, fading polaroids,
the unseen others and the unknowns
are there as well, the ancestors
who so willfully work
in the family's behalf. Ashé.

જ

The Car is the Crucial Chariot to Rural Culture

If you are twenty miles from a city, and a dance every Friday night at Hillcrest Gardens, and you live a quarter-mile from Sandy Cross crossroad and the same distance in the other direction towards Joppa Baptist Church, and Bill Jordan's joint is five miles north of there, but the Hillcrest run takes you down Low Ground Road, through the thick piney-woods, and every now a pocket of houses to the south, the swamp where the big bucks walk the hunting season, the old folk say this is a haunted piece of land on both sides of that short bridge barely big enough for two vehicles side by side, a driveway that crosses over the blackwater river, and around the curve from there, in the cornfield stubble, in the gloam, the flock of wild turkeys gleaning the grain left by the combine, the low ground route has nine graveyards, the separate blacks and whites, at night a heavy fog always rises over this road.

The Preparatory Fire for the Hog

The air is sharp, colder than the shallow river that has started
to freeze, a thin pane of ice growing just off the banks, the first
week of January when the ground is hard, and the woods, a
shame of naked trees shattered among the evergreens, deer
beds in the tall brown grass on the other side of the pig pen
fence, the enclosed grubbed field that doesn't have a root,
blade of grass or a weed, and the family is in heavy coats and
mud-boots, there is an array of sharpened knives, a prayer of
abundance, the work of harvesting pork, a twelve year-old boy
hauls firewood to the steel trough where he will heat the water
to scald the dead hog.

Absolution

It ain't like I ever lived in Eden
but understand that I do know the snake
and consider where he was coming from.
his knowledge of the underworld
and the surface too, we ain't usually
that deep into that side of the tracks.
Where we from everything is a swallow
of high proof moonshine and storms,
there's always troubles and trials,
a newspaper load to testify, but on that side
the sun shines blessings down on the tree,
a lush grass carpets their naked feet,
and they never worried, believing
they had this privilege from God,
who the snake loves, and thinks that he
also deserves so much better, so how
could he not resent them he ain't
one of the mild-mannered animals
in their sacred garden so bountiful.

Hankering

I'd left the radio on and J.D. McCloud
is playing a Mississippi flood song,

that constant heavy rain the bluesy threat
of landslides and falling trees,

the water that always wins.
It makes me think of you

from beyond old-school when
record shops had radio stations

midnight broadcasting from Memphis
all cross the south the red-light slow dance

like it was delivered by Jesus on a motorcycle,
the true gospel to the crack in the road

where I live now with our mythology.
We been off and on so long

it feels like there is a sacredness about it.
I finish my cigarette and a cup of black coffee.

I been running towards you. I keep the radio
switched on, but I turn it down, play it

low so I can hear the spirits better.
I pray to the ju-ju band. They tell me

if at this high water moment, if we
don't have a real love thing

then what we really have is nothing.

Cultivating My No Regret

I am the age when shoveling snow
can take me out and as a matter
of fact right now I do live in a barn.
Three Douglass fir trees stand
at the corner of my fence and each reaches
a hundred feet into the morning fog.
The juvenile eagles silently glide by
down the middle of this northwest world.
The peace of the lagoon and its collected snags
is right down the hill and the great herons
are already building their nests.
The seagulls have not yet started to squawk.
The crows greet each other. A dog,
not mine, who loves me, comes to howl
at my door and I come out and sit
on my small porch and watch
the sun rise over the crests of the hills
on the other side. This is where
the music starts, where I find
the holy ghost. I have more
instruments than I can actually play,
and I still have to have a banjo.

The Choices for the Pistol and the Knife

The men have gathered around the thick steel rod at the end of the trough where the fire has been built and as usual someone has a pint of shine and it is passed around as they look over the hogs all gathered in the far corner of the pen, you can see the last breaths of every chosen animal; and every man, woman, and child has a job to do, the day promises to be as cold and hard as the ground they are standing on, because having enough food can keep you from feeling like you're poor, every man wiping his mouth knows that, knows how to deal with hunger that comes from the child belly, so two of the older boys are chosen; the one with the almost-mustache and the tall one home from the Army, they will kill the hogs.

The Moonshiner's Wife

A swollen lip and a black eye ain't going to see any archangels around here. She can't take another beating, where the deacons? There ain't nobody here willing to step into the liquored sanctuary of his home and put a stop to this. Keep letting her two boys see that. I can see the hurt in their faces, the deep furrows already in their brows, I can see them hating him. They young now but they already got that man musk and I know it won't be long before one of them steps to him with piss on their hands. And I'm sorry, I don't think she want either of her boys in prison for killing his father. A drinking man is bad trouble in a family. But a drinking man with an endless supply of whiskey is the devil's continuous flow of hell-stench into the house. He blacked her eye before church service, and then later got mad and beat her again because she still went to worship, but without any make-up. Her boys, she got to save them, she don't want either of them ever treating their wives like that. She gonna have to make him quit, or kill him herself.

Snakehandler

Been the Rattlers Assistant Defensive Coach at the high school bout five years now, right after I played some college ball and used all that eligibility, never graduated, and there ain't no jobs round here and this don't pay that much but I got it, and I'm a man who always got a Bible in the hip pocket, and trying to do right coaching linebackers, play hard, play fair, no cussing, and on the bus to the championship game the team was playing that music they listen to roll of thunder loud, cause they ain't had a history of winning seasons, we so small town we ain't even a town, we farmers, them boys were singing a song where I couldn't understand a word they singing, but they were together, and I could feel their blood pumping, I could see the black warrior ghosting in their eyes, bigger and louder, and when we pulled into the stadium parking lot I told them: Get ready you dirt road folks, God-willing, tonight, we gonna shit outta these city boys, and they cranked it up again because the Lord will provide for the righteous.

Morning News from the Wheelchair Man

That dark skin girl from Haiti
they say she twenty year old
you know her she was killed
in broad daylight we going about
minding each our own damn business
whole bunch of people in a crowd
but mostly women
waiting for the 7:20 bus

She was stabbed a dozen times
but it seemed like a hundred
it's a shame to all of us that we
who was there watching scared
could do not a thing the blade flashing
the blood just flying and today
that girl is no more after stalked
by this terrible man

He want to marry her so now why
waste time we all have seen him
killing that dark skin girl who works
at the dry-cleaner on Patterson Avenue
she got a baby girl they say is not none
of his now we see him on tv news
walking goddamn puffed-up proud
in chains like he King Big-Shit

We know he the one can't they
hang this bad man what investigation
needed now it's over girl is killed dead
kill dead this man
need not waste not one damn minute
kill him during the commercial break
stab him many many times
like he stabbed the Haitian girl

Depredation

Three blocks east of the metro train,
cross a four-lane busy street
leaving the Safeway, is where Charlie
from the veterans' group got robbed,
in fucking daylight. Four bags of groceries:
corn flakes, milk, butter and eggs,
a good mess of collards, shrimp and lamb
for two meals of curry. Charlie likes meals,
so every day he cooks, says being
in his kitchen doesn't make him think of Nam.
He had ten pounds of basmati rice,
bacon, a bag of red beans and some
hickory-smoked turkey for the seasoning,
bell peppers, red and green, and yellow onions.
The bags dangling close to the ground.
Two teenagers just walked up. Skinny one
that was shaking he had the gun
pointing at Charlie's face, so he slowly
sat the bags down. He could see them both.
The other one was chewing gum.
Charlie done lived war, done run
through jungle being shot at. Gum-chewer
said give it up motherfucker, and Charlie did.
He surprised the assholes, emptied
his pockets just like that. He knew
how to get home safe. Gum-chewer

big-scowled, but took the money, shaky gun,
still surprised at how easy it all was,
asked him, what we do now?
Gum-chewer paused to think about it,
That's when Charlie got scared
and the PTSD kicked in.

Sustenance

Out the shadows of old-growth forest
to Seattle in my rolling junebug green
1994 cadillac sedan de ville
to gather a pile of wrinkled ones
and tens and five dollar bills inside
the scarred-up hardcase for my guitar,

and when I finish busking the gospel
and the blue plate special on lunch-time
Pioneer Square I find a place to sit still
and smoke a fresh organic cigarette,
my rules: never count the gift money
in the sunspot where I play,

and do not drink anything but water.
then fall into the bones, the songs
I love, the crow call music that scores
my old-school bop, my gracious ghost walk,
my cane of Rasta carved oak, and provision,
for my tribute: gas, groceries, a pack of smokes.

When the Boys were Pallbearers That Summer

The six boys on old Miss Pearl's porch were all wearing white short-sleeve shirts without ties because in late July it's too hot to wear the black suitcoats, and, except for the occasional fan of a hand towards a fly, they all stood as still as they could in the corner shaded from the pecan tree, the mortician had earlier rolled Miss Pearl into her living room, his air-conditioned hearse humming under the tree, the boys, all of whom had regularly pinched church offerings to buy the candy Miss Pearl sold between Sunday School and Sunday Service, knowing she knows, and she forgives sins, childless, her family, these siblings and cousins sweating on the porch, and across the road a crowd of fifty people waiting in the shade-less church yard, some of the men squatting under the protective brims of their fedoras, the women with parasols, and when the church bell tolled the boys went single-file into Miss Pearl's house, the clapboards faded, generations of weather, into her living room, her plastic-covered beige chair and sofa removed, her coffee table of magazines under the window, the casket on rollers in the middle of the room, and when they came out they steadied their step, the air-conditioned hearse humming under the shade tree, but they commenced to walking Miss Pearl across Joppa Road.

Whiskey

Just like I believe there is no better angel than a dog
a shot glass has an infinite capacity
to hold my sins and the marks I have against me
disappear clean and neat the burn of whiskey
the communion that finds the lost soul
the dead-letter box where all my mail goes
is washed clean by whiskey all the women
who eventually wished me gone are now
gone through the blue magic of whiskey
all those who discovered I did not earn enough
to buy endless lattes within the chatter
of the caffeine junkies discussing the going-ons
at the all night co-op have been discounted
and sit on the bottom shelf of the clearance sale
anyone who for whatever reason put me last is now
definitely last my barking savior has been a bottle
in a bar that has a juke box of whiskey songs
featuring drunken guitar players and alcoholic gals
and that is my solace my redemption
my elevator to heaven my hair of the dog.

Don't Let Your Mouth Write a Check Your Ass Can't Cash

My advice, just keep quiet,
be a swaying loblolly pine
in the distance, even if you always felt
like a shack, with blistering paint,
and a crooked chimney, in the middle
of a nowhere from a long time ago,
and maybe in this parable you lived
in High Point, a small North Carolina city,
and your neighborhood was across
the invisible tracks, or maybe across actual
steel tracks where whatever parent(s)
you had, and maybe their parents,
worked as furniture factory laborers,
running the sanders or assembling dinette chairs,
and maybe one of them once saw
some soon-to-be-sad matriarch's grandson
get shot in Matthew Johnson's liquor-house,
on a Friday night with the smell of fish grease
coming from the kitchen, maybe a shot
of bourbon neat on the card table,
a brand new deck still in the box,

maybe a long-legged gal standing behind him
rubbing her tits into his back like he was
fresh money, an unlit fat reefer hanging nasty
off his bottom lip making a lop-sided smile,
a fancy watch on his wrist, and his hands
with the rings of silver and gold busy
pulling in the pile of lost rents,
winning five pots straight, and after
letting everybody know that he ain't
got to worry about any of them
missing-teeth mo-foes messing
with him because maybe he packing.

The Marys

The five married women are in the kitchen, skillet cooking slices of fresh pork which will be the sandwiches served for lunch with cold Coca-Cola; they laugh and joke about their husbands to the other wives, but nobody talks about any husband but their own, that is their code, no mentions of drunks, beaters or ramblers, never recollections of other lovers lest his name be Jesus, and the loudest woman is already working on the evening meal, more fresh pork, macaroni and cheese, string beans from the fall canning, pear preserves and scratch biscuits for desert, coffee with sugar and cream, the kitchen windows sweating from all the contained heat.

The Granddaughters and the Queen-Mother

The young women, and the girls, clean the guts delivered by the washtub-full, blooded and blue-tinted ropes steaming the unfinished business of the pig into the overcast day, a stab of stench to soon be gone, bucket after the bucket of cold water, and they are delivered translucent and clean to the matriarch who sits at a wooden work table set in the yard, where the boy has built a fire nearby, and she grinds the fresh pig meat, adds the salt, black pepper, a touch of nutmeg, the sage, sprinkles of parsley and red pepper flakes, packs it all and creates the links of sausage, the savory chain of before-sunrise breakfasts that will hang from the rafters of the smokehouse.

They Tell Me

They tell me the night it happened there was a waning moon giving just enough light over the house, the peeling white clapboard that her deceased husband had built, and Mary could clearly see that it was the Lumbee, Jim Pierce, in her front yard, drunk, stumbling and cussing and calling out for, Elnora, her 15 year old daughter. All the crickets had ceased their chirping. Eva, Elnora's four year old cousin, was holding tightly to Mary's gown and uncontrollably trembling. They were all standing in the kitchen area of the house.

Mary had earlier turned down the kerosene lamp, as she usually does after she'd read a chapter in her Bible. Now, she blew the lamp completely out, plunging the house into a total darkness that took their eyes a few long seconds to adjust enough to see each other. But in that space of darkness they could hear the dreadful rhythms of their collective hurried breaths, a quickening but soft percussive song of distress. They were all barefoot on the smooth wooden floor in their white flannel nightgowns. They tell me you could have mistaken them as baptismal candidates.

There was a stark luminance in the gray stands of Mary's short hair, her face was drawn tight, she looked at the girls: Elnora, a near-woman teenager that she'd recently heard was starting to seriously flirt and now Jim Pierce is drunk and nasty in the yard; and he was terrifying Eva like he was some kind of red-

21

eyed demon from the dark woods, a drunk logwood man on payday, her mouth balled-up in a low volume cry, Both of them, their eyes wide and searching her eyes. Mary reached out and touched them both. "Trust in God," she told the girls. They tell me this was a Christian house, there was a Bible beside every bed.

Jim Pierce stomped up the porch and was pounding at the door. None of them were speaking. Elnora looked at her mother and glanced towards the cabinet. Mary moved there and ran her hand across the top shelf for the .45 her son George had brought home from Germany.

They tell me George didn't ever sleep much, after he'd taken up his father's trade making moonshine, and that the only time he didn't carry that military gun was when he was working at the still. The sheriffs don't like it if you get caught at a still and you got a gun. Old Sheriff Henry Wilkes might give you a chance and not shoot you, but not one of his deputies, including his son Hank, was going do that for any black man. The gun wasn't there.

They tell me Mary called out, You best stop all this fool behavior Jim Pierce you more than twice that girl's age my boys be home presently and I don't want them hurting nobody and getting in trouble or into mess that might involve the law go home now. And they tell me he answered back, Ohhh, they aint coming any time soon, he said, they each got an arm wrapped 'round one them Joppa women. After this bold clarifying statement Jim Pierce quieted down and let that sink in. Then he went to the edge of the porch and threw-up in the yard. He pulled a pint bottle from his back pocket, drank the last of it to rinse his mouth, swallowed and dropped the empty into the puke.

About the Author

GARY COPELAND LILLEY is originally from North Carolina and now lives in the Pacific Northwest. He is published in numerous anthologies and journals, including *Best American Poetry 2014*, *Willow Springs*, *Waxwing*, the *Taos International Journal of Poetry*, and the *African American Review*. He is a Cave Canem Fellow.

www.ingramcontent.com/pod-product-compliance
Lightning Source LLC
Chambersburg PA
CBHW032108040426
42449CB00007B/1221